DATE DUE

EDGE BOOKS

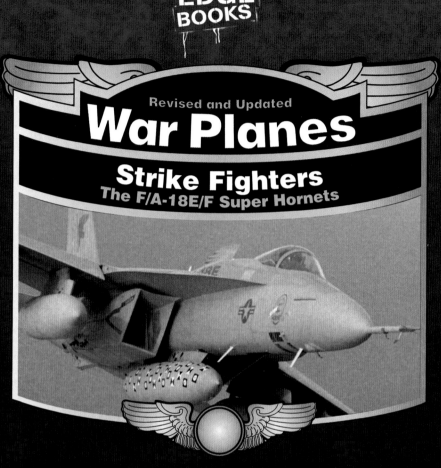

Revised and Updated

War Planes

Strike Fighters
The F/A-18E/F Super Hornets

by Bill Sweetman

Consultant:
Raymond L. Puffer, PhD, Historian
Air Force Flight Test Center
Edwards Air Force Base, California

Capstone
press

Mankato, Minnesota

Edge Books are published by Capstone Press,
151 Good Counsel Drive, P.O. Box 669, Mankato, Minnesota 56002.
www.capstonepress.com

Library of Congress Cataloging-in-Publication Data
Sweetman, Bill.
    Strike fighters : the F/A-18E/F Super Hornets / by Bill Sweetman — Rev. and
updated.
        p. cm. — (Edge books. War planes)
    Includes bibliographical references and index.
    ISBN-13: 978-1-4296-1317-0 (hardcover)
    ISBN-10: 1-4296-1317-3 (hardcover)
    1. Hornet (Jet fighter plane) — Juvenile literature. I. Title. II. Series.
UG1242.F5S962 2008
623.74'63 — dc22   2007031333

Summary: Introduces the Super Hornets, their missions, equipment, weapons,
    and use in the military.

Editorial Credits
Matt Doeden, editor; Katy Kudela, revised edition editor and photo researcher;
    Kyle Grenz, revised edition designer

Photo Credits
Boeing Management Company, 23
DVIC/TSGT Rob Tabor, USAF, cover
Ted Carlson/Fotodynamics, 9, 10, 13, 16–17, 18, 24, 27, 29
U.S. Navy photo, 1, 4, 7, 21

1 2 3 4 5 6 13 12 11 10 09 08

Table of Contents

The Super Hornet in Action

Learn about
- Carrier takeoff
- The Super Hornet's mission
- Differences from the Hornet

The aircraft carrier USS *Abraham Lincoln* moves through the water at 25 miles (40 kilometers) per hour. A gray Super Hornet fighter plane moves slowly on the front of the ship's huge deck.

Crewmembers hook a steel launch bar to the plane's front right wheel. The other end of the bar rests in a long slot in the deck. Steam hisses from the slot.

The pilot brings the plane's engines to full power. But the plane does not move. A second steel bar on the plane's rear holds it to the deck. This bar is called the holdback bar. Behind the plane, large steel panels tilt up. This blast deflector forces the jet engine's exhaust gases up and away from the deck.

The carrier's cat officer is in charge of the plane's launch. The pilot salutes to signal that he is ready to take off. The cat officer makes sure everything is ready. He then signals to begin the launch of the plane.

Another crewmember flips a switch. Steam from the aircraft's engines bursts into the **catapult**. The catapult pulls on the launch bar. The holdback bar unlatches. The Super Hornet rockets forward. It reaches a speed of more than 150 miles (241 kilometers) per hour in two seconds. The plane quickly climbs into the air. The pilot is ready to begin his mission.

catapult — a device used to launch airplanes from the deck of an aircraft carrier

About the Super Hornet

The F/A-18E/F Super Hornet is a carrier aircraft. It can take off from and land on aircraft carriers. The Super Hornet is the U.S. Navy's newest carrier aircraft.

The Super Hornet carries bombs, missiles, and a cannon. Pilots use these fighter planes to attack ground targets, enemy ships, or other aircraft.

The U.S. Navy began using the Super Hornet in 1995. Today, the Navy uses two models of the airplane. Boeing builds both models. The E model has only one seat. The F model includes a second seat behind the pilot.

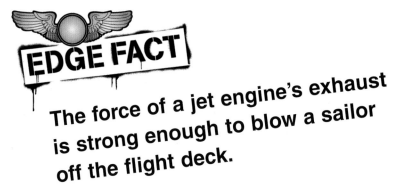

EDGE FACT

The force of a jet engine's exhaust is strong enough to blow a sailor off the flight deck.

The Super Hornet is a large, powerful strike fighter.

The Super Hornet is based on earlier designs of the F/A-18 Hornet. The Navy first used this aircraft in 1983. The Hornet was an important fighter plane during the Gulf War (1991).

The Super Hornet is about 25 percent bigger than the Hornet. It has larger wings and more powerful engines. The Super Hornet carries more weapons and fuel than the Hornet. It can even refuel other planes during flight.

Inside the Super Hornet

Learn about

- Body design
- Engine power
- Head-up display (HUD)

The Super Hornet is a large fighter plane. It is 60 feet, 3 inches (18.5 meters) long. The Super Hornet has broad, straight wings. It has two rear wings called horizontal stabilators. The stabilators help the pilot control the plane at high speeds. The Super Hornet also has two vertical rudders attached to the plane's rear. The rudders help the pilot make tight turns. They also help the pilot control the plane's nose when it is pointing up.

Landing and Takeoff Equipment

The Super Hornet needs equipment to take off from and land on aircraft carriers. Carrier landings are especially difficult for pilots. Wind and waves can make landing a challenge. Super Hornets do not have enough room to stop normally on a carrier deck. They need extra help to stop in time.

A Super Hornet pilot flies straight toward the carrier deck to land. A hook on the plane's tail must connect with a steel cable stretched across the carrier deck. This cable is called an arrester wire. The arrester wire pulls against the hook. This action quickly slows down the plane. The plane's front wheels then slam into the deck. The Super Hornet comes to a full stop in less than two seconds.

EDGE FACT

A Super Hornet's landing on a ship is sometimes called a "controlled crash."

Strong landing gear helps Super Hornets stop quickly.

Carrier decks are too short for standard takeoffs. Super Hornets have launch bars that attach to catapults. The catapults use power from the carrier's steam engines to pull planes quickly up to flying speed. Planes could not take off from carriers without this extra speed.

Engines

The Super Hornet is powered by two jet engines. Each engine provides 22,000 pounds (9,977 kilograms) of thrust. The Super Hornet can reach speeds of more than 1,300 miles (2,100 kilometers) per hour.

Pilot Controls

The Super Hornet has many controls and instruments inside its cockpit. Pilots use the controls to fly the planes. Pilots use instruments to keep track of the planes' speed, location, and weapons.

The Super Hornet's main controls are the control stick and the throttle. Pilots steer their planes with the control stick and rudders. Pilots control their planes' speed with the throttle. Many controls and buttons are located on the stick and throttle. Pilots use these controls to operate Super Hornet systems without removing their hands from the stick or throttle.

F/A-18E/F Specifications

Function:	Multi-role attack and fighter aircraft
Manufacturer:	Boeing (formerly McDonnell Douglas)
Deployed:	1995
Length:	60 feet, 3 inches (18.5 meters)
Wingspan:	44 feet, 9 inches (13.7 meters)
Height:	16 feet (4.9 meters)
Max. Weight:	66,000 pounds (29,932 kilograms)
Payload:	17,750 pounds (8,032 kilograms)
Engine:	Two F414-GE-400 turbofan engines
Thrust:	22,000 pounds (9,977 kilograms) per engine
Speed:	1,300 miles (2,100 kilometers) per hour
Ceiling:	50,000 feet (15,240 meters)
Combat Range:	1,465 miles (2,358 kilometers)

Most of the Super Hornet's instruments are in the front of the cockpit. A head-up display (HUD) is also located in front of the pilot. The HUD screen allows the pilot to see flight information. The pilot can look at the HUD without looking down at the cockpit controls.

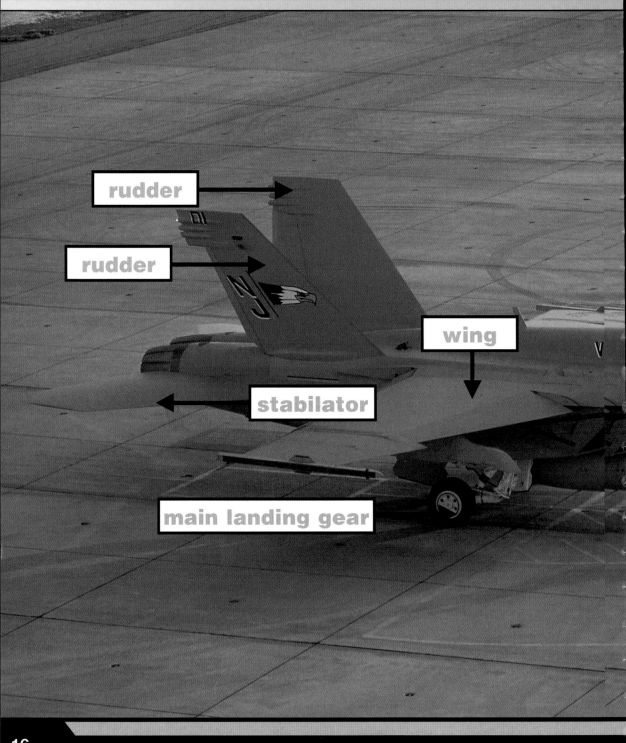

rudder

rudder

wing

stabilator

main landing gear

cockpit

VFA-122

101

center line tank

nose landing gear

Weapons and Tactics

Learn about

- Sidewinder missiles
- Laser-guided bombs
- Defensive weapons

The Super Hornet carries a variety of weapons to help pilots complete missions. The weight of a Super Hornet's weapons and equipment is called the payload. Pilots use a M61A1 Vulcan cannon, missiles, and bombs to attack ground targets and enemy aircraft. The number and kinds of weapons a Super Hornet carries depend on the pilot's mission.

Cannons and Air-to-Air Missiles

All Super Hornets carry a six-barrel M61A1 Vulcan in the plane's nose. It can fire 100 shells per second. Pilots use these cannons mainly against enemy aircraft.

The Super Hornet often carries air-to-air missiles for combat with other aircraft. The AIM-9 Sidewinder is one common missile. The Super Hornet carries Sidewinders on the tips of its wings. The Sidewinder is effective in close combat. It includes a heat-seeking device in its nose. This equipment guides the Sidewinder toward sources of heat such as the exhaust from enemy planes.

The Super Hornet also carries the AIM-120 AMRAAM. AMRAAM is short for "Advanced Medium-Range Air-to-Air Missile." Pilots often call these missiles "Slammers." The AIM-120 includes a built-in **radar** system.

radar — equipment that uses radio waves to locate and guide objects

Navy members load shells for the F/A-18's cannon.

Surface Weapons

Super Hornet pilots sometimes attack enemy ships. The Super Hornet carries a missile called a Harpoon for these missions. The Harpoon missile is powered by a small jet engine. The Harpoon has a large warhead that explodes when the missile hits its target.

The SLAM (Stand-off Land Attack Missile) is a version of the Harpoon. Pilots use the SLAM against targets on land. The SLAM includes a camera and a radio control link. The missile sends a picture through the radio control link. The pilot can use this picture to choose the exact spot for the missile to strike.

Laser-guided bombs (LGBs) are another surface weapon. Super Hornet pilots aim a laser beam at a target. They then release the LGBs. The LGBs have sensors that detect the laser. The bombs then fly toward the target.

Defensive Weapons

Some Super Hornet weapons are designed to protect the plane from enemy missiles. Enemies may use surface-to-air missiles (SAMs) to destroy Super Hornets.

The Super Hornet carries the AGM-88 High-Speed Anti-Radiation Missile (HARM). This missile can seek out and destroy enemy radar equipment. Without radar guidance, an enemy's SAM will fly off course.

The Super Hornet carries a variety of missiles.

The AGM-154 Joint Stand-Off Weapon (JSOW) is another defensive weapon. The JSOW is a gliding weapon. It has no engine. The JSOW glides to its target and releases 145 small bombs. These bombs can destroy enemy missile launchers and other targets.

Serving the Military

Learn about
- Towed decoys
- Radar jamming
- Future plans

The Super Hornet is one of the Navy's newest and most effective airplanes. Navy officials are pleased with the Super Hornet's performance. But they also know that the plane can be better. The Navy has already made some improvements to the Super Hornet. These improvements help the Super Hornet remain one of the best and most modern planes in service.

New Defenses

New Super Hornets may carry a **towed decoy** to protect it from SAMs. The decoy is a small dart on the end of a long cable. The cable is attached to the plane's rear. The dart sends out electronic signals designed to confuse SAM radar. SAM radar may see the dart and the plane as a single target. SAMs then would be aimed at the center of the combined target. These missiles would miss the plane.

The Navy plans to buy a special version of the Super Hornet to attack enemy radar stations. These planes will carry electronic devices to help pilots detect enemy radar. Pilots then will be able to aim powerful radio signals at enemy radar stations. These signals prevent radar from working properly. This action is called "jamming." Enemy troops at radar stations would not be able to use radar to aim missiles. Radar jamming would keep Super Hornet pilots safe from SAM attacks.

towed decoy — a device that sends out electronic signals to confuse enemy radar

Future Usefulness

The Navy has no plans to replace the Super Hornet in the near future. New computers, radar devices, and weapons will keep the Super Hornet up to date.

The Super Hornet is fast and powerful. It can make quick turns. It can carry a variety of weapons. No other U.S. military aircraft can perform all of the Super Hornet's missions. The Super Hornet will remain an important part of the military for many years to come.

EDGE FACT

The Navy buys about 50 new Super Hornets each year.

GLOSSARY

arrester wire (uh-REST-uhr WIRE) — a steel cable that is stretched across an aircraft carrier's deck

catapult (KAT-uh-puhlt) — a device used to launch airplanes from the deck of an aircraft carrier

laser beam (LAY-zur BEEM) — a narrow, intense beam of light

radar (RAY-dar) — equipment that uses radio waves to locate and guide objects

rudder (RUHD-ur) — a metal plate attached to a plane to help the pilot steer

stabilator (STAY-buh-lay-tuhr) — the rear wing of an airplane

thrust (THRUHST) — the force created by a jet engine; thrust pushes an airplane forward.

towed decoy (TOHD DEE-koi) — a device that sends out electronic signals to confuse enemy radar

READ MORE

Anderson, Jameson. *Fighter Pilot.* Atomic. Chicago: Raintree, 2007.

Bledsoe, Karen E. *Fighter Planes: Fearless Fighters.* Mighty Military Machines. Berkeley Heights, N.J.: Enslow, 2006.

Zuehlke, Jeffrey. *Fighter Planes.* Pull Ahead Books. Minneapolis: Lerner, 2006.

INTERNET SITES

FactHound offers a safe, fun way to find Internet sites related to this book. All of the sites on FactHound have been researched by our staff.

Here's how:
1. Visit *www.facthound.com*
2. Choose your grade level.
3. Type in this book ID **1429613173** for age-appropriate sites. You may also browse subjects by clicking on letters, or by clicking on pictures and words.
4. Click on the **Fetch It** button.

FactHound will fetch the best sites for you!

INDEX